Through the eyes of me

This book belongs to:

'Delightfully told and beautifully illustrated, Through the Eyes of Me will help siblings, classmates and anyone who knows a child on the autism spectrum.' **Alex White, Scope**

'A beautiful story about a beautiful girl. We hope others love Kya's story as much as we do.' **National Autistic Association Cymru**

'This beautiful and charming book captures the true delights of being autistic.'
Alan Gardner, The Autistic Gardener

'What a lovely book – it gets the understanding across whilst showing the normality and uniqueness of Kya. I would love to read this to my children one day.'
Amy Willerton, TV presenter and model

'This beautifully illustrated book describes the world as perceived by a very young child who has autism. The text eloquently explains why she is different to her peers and will educate and entertain the reader. This is a work of art, love and understanding.'
Professor Tony Attwood

'Through the eyes of me is a great children's book that looks at what life is like for Kya as a young autistic girl. It's done in a simple, easy to follow and extremely positive way that I feel could be helpful to other autistic children and many children in general to simply understand autism.' **Alex Lowery, Autistic Public speaker and trainer on autism**

Through the Eyes of Me.
Published in Great Britain in 2017 by Graffeg Limited

Written by Jon Roberts copyright © 2017.
Illustrated by Hannah Rounding copyright © 2017.
Designed and produced by Graffeg Limited copyright © 2017

Graffeg Limited, 24 Stradey Park Business Centre, Mwrwg Road, Llangennech, Llanelli, Carmarthenshire SA14 8YP Wales UK Tel 01554 824000 www.graffeg.com

Jon Roberts is hereby identified as the author of this work in accordance with section 77 of the Copyrights, Designs and Patents Act 1988.

A CIP Catalogue record for this book is available from the British Library.

ISBN 9781912213009

1 2 3 4 5 6 7 8 9

Through the eyes of me

Jon Roberts

Illustrations Hannah Rounding

GRAFFEG

I am always on the move,

I don't care for sitting still.

I often make my mummy
and daddy very tired.

I love running,

but I don't quite understand life's dangers and my
mummy and daddy need to make sure I am safe.

I love it when my daddy lifts me high in the air

and spins me around and around and around and around

It makes me feel so happy.

I love being tickled, especially when my mummy blows raspberries on my belly.

Mummy says that

my smile makes everyone happy

and that

my laughter is infectious.

I don't look at you in the eye when
you speak to me, but

I am listening to you
and I am absorbing your every word.

I will surprise you most days when I suddenly say a new word for the first time.

Be sure to say my name before speaking to me so I know you are talking to me.

I love singing songs, especially nursery rhymes.

But sometimes, when *the volume is a bit loud,*
I cover my ears to block out the noise.

My ears are *sensitive to sound.*

I enjoy playing alongside my school friends, but I haven't learnt how to join in the games yet.

I find it *difficult* communicating.

I love reading books and looking at stickers.
But be careful, I also enjoy ripping them up.

I like sorting toys out on the floor.
Sometimes

I line them up.

Sometimes I order them into groups

and sometimes

I
stack
them
on
top
of
each
other.

This gives me
comfort

and a sense
of control.

I don't like many foods. If I don't like the look of it
or it *feels funny*, I will push the food away.

I love chicken nuggets and ice cream.

My mummy and daddy wish I would
eat some vegetables.

I love looking at myself in the mirror and...

Pulling funny faces.

I often stare at a favourite picture and go into daydreams.

Mummy and daddy think I am...

daydreaming about ice cream.

I love **spinning** around on the spot.

I quite often

tippy toe

around

if I am unsure

about something.

I love jumping up and down

and

waving my arms

with excitement.

I would be a
fantastic ballerina.

Did I mention
I love running?

I am autistic.

I am Kya.

Jon Roberts

This book was written by Jon Roberts as a dedication to his beautiful, creative, loving and ever surprising daughter, Kya.

It is hoped that other people whose lives are affected by the joys and challenges of autism, either directly or indirectly, may be able to identify and connect with this story.

As human beings, we are all unique and precious, and should embrace and love those differences with all our heart and being.

Useful links

Autism

Alex Lowery
www.alexlowery.co.uk

Ambitious About Autism
www.ambitiousaboutautism.org.uk

Autistica
www.autistica.org.uk

Autism Aware
www.autismaware.co.uk

Autism Awareness
www.autismawareness.com.au

Autism Education Trust
www.autismeducationtrust.org.uk

Autism NI
www.autismni.org

Autism Plus
www.autismplus.org

Autism Research Centre
www.autismresearchcentre.com

Child Autism
www.childautism.org.uk

Leeds ABC Support Group
www.abcleeds.org.uk/contact.php

National Autistic Society
www.autism.org.uk

PDA Society
www.pdasociety.org.uk

The PDA Resource
www.thepdaresource.com

Research Autism
www.researchautism.net

Scottish Autism
www.scottishautism.org

General

Cerebra
w3.cerebra.org.uk

Contact a Family
www.cafamily.org.uk

Family Fund
www.familyfund.org.uk

The Growing Zone
www.growingzone.co.uk

Home-Start UK
www.home-start.org.uk

I Can
www.ican.org.uk

IPSEA
www.ipsea.org.uk

Scope
www.scope.org.uk

Sibs
www.sibs.org.uk

SNAP
www.snapcymru.org

Young Minds
www.youngminds.org.uk